IMPROBABLE MENTORS
&
HAPPY TANGENTS

Improbable Mentors

&

Happy Tangents
(Edition One)

How firefighters and poets, truckers and nurses,
soldiers and singers, and other improbable individuals
can show you the way in business and creativity

Michael Perry

Cover design: RT Vrieze, Knorth Studios
Paperback ISBN: 979-8-9856638-5-3
eBook ISBN: 979-8-9856638-3-9
Audiobook ISBN: 979-8-9856638-4-6

Contents

Author's note

Whatever happened to me?

I had always been a sensible young fellow. A tad drifty, often lost in books, and prone to clowning my way out of trouble, but otherwise well grounded in the rural working-class world of my childhood. My parents were solid, faithful, and loving. My siblings and I were given responsibilities and expected to meet them. Drove my first tractor at the age of nine. Ran my first pitchfork long before that.

I got good grades and got into college. Went for a nursing degree. Slightly unusual for a knuckleheaded farm boy, but vocationally viable. Practical.

Even in love I remained focused on the pragmatic path. When my long-time girlfriend broached the subject of marriage, I solemnly declared I wasn't going to start a family until I had my degree and my first job.

Sensible. Practical.

I did get that degree. I did get that first job.

Pragmatic.

And then I pitched it all and took off on a tangent that turned into another tangent that turned into other tangents that are still spinning into new tangents. For three decades now I've been my own boss, meeting, working with, and writing about fascinating, insightful, tenacious, quirky, famous, unknown, and inspirational people of all stripes and stations.

It's a life I never anticipated. A life that has allowed me experiences and opportunities I never saw coming when I was stacking hay bales in rural Wisconsin.

And it's a life that never would have happened without my mentors.

My *improbable* mentors. The ones who showed me the way. The *way*. Not the *path*.

The path you gotta make on your own. But when you accumulate advice from a broad range of folks beyond and outside your area of so-called expertise, those folks are showing you the *ways* things can be done—no matter what you choose to do.

* * *

This little book grew out of a talk I was asked to prepare describing my most improbable mentors and the lessons they taught me about how to thrive and survive where the worlds of art and business overlap. Portions of the manuscript draw on pieces I wrote for *Men's Health* magazine, the books *Danger: Man Working*, *Off Main Street*, *Visiting Tom*, and *Population 485*, and a writing memoir in progress.

* * *

That girlfriend and I are still friendly. We never did get married. We went off on our own tangents.

PART ONE:
MINDING YOUR MENTORS,
CHASING YOUR TANGENTS

Happiness Is a Warm Cannon

I ONCE WROTE A *NEW YORK TIMES* BESTSELLING BOOK about my neighbor Tom. Tom never went to college. Been farming all his life. Builds his own cannons from scratch. *Real* cannons. Cannons that wobble my windows from two miles away. Cannons so big that when he's outta cannon balls he shoots beef stew cans filled with concrete.

Tom overflows with roughneck wisdom. You can learn more about life and persistence from following him around his farm for a day than you'll learn in a semester at some of your leading academic institutions or a week of business hype seminars. Rough as a cob but whip-smart and well-read, he's the walking definition of a self-taught genius. If you ask him how to make moonshine or black powder, or convert an industrial generator into a portable welder, or build a sawmill from scratch, or turn an axle spindle on a lathe, he'll have read up on it, and he'll have done it.

Tom's knowledge extends beyond the practical into the philosophical. It has to. He's a father. Raised two daughters. Was married for sixty years to a woman he courted on a 1948 Harley Davidson. Watched as his beloved farm—his only home for all of his 90-plus years—was split in two when the state plowed a four-lane interstate through his front yard. He went from birdsong mornings to 24,000 vehicles a day blasting past so close the dishes tremble in the cupboard. And yet he never retreated into cynicism or self-pity. Instead he just kept working and building and creating and taking his joy where he found it—including with that cannon.

Whenever we had visitors from out of town, we'd take them to Tom's place. He loved nothing more than rolling that cannon out of the shed, charging it with a big wad of homemade black powder, ramming a projectile in place, inserting the fuse, and then—as his audience plugged their ears—touching it off. There'd be a rib-rattling boom, a geyser of dirt and splintered wood up in the distant tree line, and, as the cloud bank of smoke cleared, there stood Tom, his grin as big and bright as that muzzle flash.

Wrong Question, Right Answer

I SPENT THE BETTER PART OF TWO YEARS following Tom while writing my book, shadowing him as he worked, visiting at his kitchen table, and just generally observing and listening. When the manuscript was complete, we had one final sit-down to review the entire thing. Check all the details, make sure I got his story straight.

After I flipped the last page face-down, we sat quietly for a moment. Then it hit me: This could be our last visit. My final chance to gain one more nugget of insight.

I took a breath.

"Tom," I said, gesturing at the manuscript. "All these experiences. All these joys and disappointments. All these things you've learned. All this *living*."

I could hear the traffic roaring just outside the farmhouse as I carefully composed one last question.

"Do you have any regrets?"

Tom looked me squarely in the eye and answered just as squarely.

"Yep."

The traffic rumbled unabated for nearly half a minute, until I realized: That was it. That was his complete and final answer.

Of *course* Tom had regrets.

But he wasn't about to share them with me!

And in that moment, Tom taught me a valuable lesson: asking a wise person for wisdom is like pushing a rope. You're going about it backwards. If you do get anything, it'll likely be all bunched up and useless, more likely to trip you up than pull you up.

The same lesson applies to choosing your mentors.

The Best Mentor I Never Met

THROUGH A SERIES OF HAPPY ACCIDENTS I wound up writing books for a living. Those books sold in part because I wrote about fascinating folks like Tom. But they also sold because they found an audience that liked my writer's *voice*—how I sounded on the page, I guess you could say.

New writers are told how important it is to establish their writing voice—and yet nothing reads worse than a writer trying to assert their voice before it is fully formed.

One of my top five writing mentors, and the one who most shaped my voice, was a man named Jim Harrison.

Whom I never met.

And who—thank goodness—was of no help at all until I was eight years into my writing career.

I had been surviving by writing whatever it took. Magazine articles and essays, but also advertising brochures, radio scripts for used car dealers, and goofy little self-help booklets. Hardly fine art, but I was learning the craft. Learning how to cut my stuff to fit, learning not to be precious about it, learning to *listen* to what I was putting on the page.

I was paying the rent, but barely.

Then—eight years in—I read a book of Jim Harrison's essays. There was something in his style, his cadence, his line breaks that spoke to me in a way no other writer had.

I began integrating his style into my own. Mimicking him, you bet, and stealing a few moves, but more than that, weaving what I'd learned from him into what I'd learned from all that "whatever it took" writing.

Within two years I had a New York City agent.

Within three years I had a book deal.

And I haven't looked back. Not because I chased down a mentor, but because that mentor found *me*. If I had met Jim Harrison in those early years, I wouldn't have known what to ask him. If I had read him in those early years, I would have missed the point. Been unready for the lessons.

When I speak on the topic to aspiring writers, I tell them that rather than finding my writer's voice, I let it find me. I had to write in many different styles. Read writers of many different styles. Read my own writing aloud. Listen to myself. Listen for clinkers. False notes. Then start tweaking. Making adjustments. In musician terms, I was learning riffs. Practicing scales. In business terms, I was compiling a spreadsheet. A list of contacts. Standard operating procedures. It isn't until later that you learn how to make it all sing.

Wait. Not *make* it all sing—*let* it all sing.

What I tell those students is, in my experience, finding my writer's "voice"—the one that has allowed me this career—was a *passive* rather than *active* process.

And I maintain the same declaration holds true in finding life-changing mentors.

You don't *ask* someone to be your mentor.

You *realize* someone is your mentor.

Take Off on a Tangent

I ONCE WROTE THAT WE SPRING FROM A THICKET OF TANGENTS. As proof, a decade after I typed that line, a woman approached me backstage at a music festival and hiked up her sleeve. There, tattooed into her arm, was that very phrase.

So many storylines make sense only when traced in reverse. In 1989 the editor of a local magazine asked me to write a piece about a band from northern Wisconsin. Having never heard of them I assumed they played taverns and polkas. Turned out they had just signed a major country music recording deal. I interviewed them, submitted the story and thought nothing more of it. Time passed, and the entertainment reporter of our local newspaper received a call from the national editor of *Country Weekly*, asking if the reporter was available to cover a nearby country music festival. Already swamped with writing up every cultural event in the Chippewa Valley from the community theater production of *Cinderella* to the high school Christmas concert, the reporter declined.

"Do you know of anyone else in the area who writes about country music?" asked the *Country Weekly* editor.

"Yes…" said the local reporter, having seen the only piece I had ever written on the subject. Next thing I knew my phone rang. It was the *Country Weekly* editor, calling from Nashville.

"Are you the guy who writes about country music?"

"*Yes. I. Am.*" When you freelance, there is only ever one answer.

The assignment that followed—a simple 300-word report— led to decades of writing about country music, music and musicians in general, and the business side of music. I accompanied bands on tours in big shiny buses, scribbled notes backstage and in recording studios, and observed countless concerts from the wings. I profiled famous artists and non-famous artists, but also the bus drivers and truckers hauling the shows down the road. I interviewed studio hands and guitar techs, roadies and managers, and anyone connected with the process. For a good decade (culminating in my interviewing country superstar Tim McGraw for a *Men's Health* magazine cover story as he ate kale salad in a makeup chair) roughly half of my income could be traced back through a thicket of tangents sprung from that one time I thought I was gonna write up a one-off on a polka band.

IMPROBABLE MENTORS, IMPROBABLE PATHS

I'VE NEVER GONE TO SCHOOL FOR WHAT I DO. You're reading the words of a farm boy with a nursing degree. I've made a good living mostly from writing books and essays and scripts but also from speaking to groups ranging from the local library to national corporations and performing as a humorist and singer. Been doing it for decades, through the ups and downs of the economy, the fragmentation and decline of the music and publishing industry, the disintegration of the human attention span, and despite being pretty much unknown.

That's neither a brag nor a self-deprecation. It's just been my path. And along that path some of my most important mentors have been what you'd expect—English professors, editors, and other writers—but the ones who contributed the most to helping me not only survive but thrive, would at first glance have nothing to do with what I do for a living.

These are my *improbable mentors*.

And the thing about improbable mentors? You carom off them into that thicket of tangents, where chance encounters lead to chance opportunities.

Opportunities that can propel you for a lifetime, no matter your craft or occupation.

In Business Terms…

• **Embrace improbable mentors and unplanned lessons:** The most valuable insights often come from unconventional sources; consult the experts but stay open to learning from diverse experiences and individuals.

• **Cultivate success in the unexpected:** Seemingly minor opportunities or side projects can lead to unexpected career breakthroughs; flexibility and curiosity are essential for long-term growth.

• **Mastery develops through experience, not instant answers:** Finding your unique expertise or niche is a process of exploration and refinement over time, rather than something that can be taught directly or rushed.

Part Two:
When Oprah Calls

Hold the Phone

My most famous improbable mentor ever was Oprah Winfrey, who taught me an everlasting lesson by proxy.

This was back in the era of her monstrously successful daily television show. If you were a writer and you could get booked on *The Oprah Winfrey Show*, it changed your life.

I was a writer.

Or trying to be one.

Oprah asked me to be on her show.

I said no.

Late one night in the early 1990s, I was driving through the northern Wisconsin darkness when my headlights illuminated a body sprawled on the road.

I pulled to a stop, hit the flashers, grabbed my rescue kit, and ran to the body.

It was a man. Bloody and unconscious. Breathing raggedly.

I cleared his airway, applied oxygen, and stopped the bleeding as best I could.

It was a long time before the ambulance arrived and took him away.

A few miles up the road I stopped at a small gas station to wash my hands. I had been wearing rubber gloves, but one of them had torn, and there was blood on my finger. I scrubbed it with soap and water and went on my way.

The next day a sheriff's deputy called me. The man had died.

"Any chance you got blood on you?" the deputy asked.

"I did," I said, at which point the deputy informed me that the man was HIV positive.

At the time, any mention of AIDS often triggered jokes, condemnation, or fear—or a combination of all three. Facing a year of testing and hoping to dispel some of the mythology—and admitting I was scared—I wrote an essay about my experience from the viewpoint of a rural EMT.

The essay was published in *Newsweek*. This was a big deal for me. I'd never written for a publication anywhere near that size. The week it came out I got a call from one of Oprah's producers.

"Oprah *loves* your essay," gushed the producer. "She wants you to come on the show and talk about it."

My heart ticked up a few beats. Me on the *Oprah* show! This could be my ticket. I'd be going nationwide. Oprah could shine a bright light on this important issue. On a less idealistic level, I also knew how many people in the New York City publishing world watched Oprah, hoping to discover the next great book idea. How could they resist me?

"We're doing a show about *heroes*," the producer said.

I felt the sand hit my gears. My excitement dropped a notch.

I wanted so badly to say yes. I was a struggling self-published writer, hungry for any break I might catch. This was the biggest of the big leagues.

"But it's not a piece about heroism," I said. "It's a piece about AIDS not just being a big city thing. About trying to educate myself about it. And I'm *nervous*, not *brave*."

"Well *we* think you're a hero!"

"I just did what I was supposed to do." Even as I said it I knew it was a cliché. But I meant it. "Same as if the person *didn't* have AIDS. And I didn't even know he was infected until after the fact. I'm happy to come on the show, but I wouldn't be comfortable coming on the show and being called a hero."

And then there I was in my little apartment, holding a phone with no one on the other end. Oprah's was an efficient crew—I figure by the time I placed the headset back in the cradle that producer had drawn a line through my name and was already dialing the next available hero.

When Yes Can Be a Mess

RE-READING WHAT I JUST SHARED, I'm aware it comes off as a deep humble-brag. So lemme be crystal clear: I *really* wanted to be on that show. And not simply for noble health-education reasons. Even as the call ended I was wracking my brain for any angle to justify calling back to say yes. And to this day I wonder if I shoulda just shut up and showed up. Taken the shot. Maybe maybe possibly gotten that big publishing deal. Coulda been the tangent of all tangents.

But I've never lost sleep over my decision. It wasn't all about altruism. And with every passing year I've grown more certain that I mighta thought I was ready for a break, but I'm pretty sure I wasn't. I likely wouldn't have known what to do with the opportunity. Or how to get the most out of it. Artistically speaking, I was still finding my voice—and frankly, didn't have much to *say* yet.

To a crasser point, I had nothing to sell yet. I'd put out a couple of self-published books, but their amateurish production and content likely would have done more to hurt my career than boost it. They were an important early step, but very much—as one reviewer put it—"an early effort."

I've already said that when you're a freelancer—or self-employed in any endeavor—the only answer is *yes*. The editor of

Backpacker magazine calls and asks if I can climb Mt. Rainier. *Yes*, I say—even though I've never climbed much more than a stepladder—because the mortgage is due. But also because I know he's less interested in my mountaineering skills than my writing skills. And that the Rainier tangent will likely lead to other tangents.

But just because opportunity knocks doesn't mean you run out the door. The timing must be right. The preparation must be in place.

In the Oprah situation, I simply wasn't comfortable with how I was being preemptively framed. I'm no purist—remember, I've written used car ads to pay the rent—but sometimes it's best to heed that inner voice. Or that visceral unease.

Know Your Palette

My Oprah experience reminds me of a quote by the German theologian and philosopher Friedrich Schleiermacher: "Whoever would make of himself a distinctive individual must be keen to perceive what he is not." Two or three times a year, my booking agent is approached by someone looking to hire my band to play their annual fire department dance. My booker knows we're always hunting gigs, but even if the department can hit our budget, we decline.

On the face of it, it seems a perfect match. I've spent the better part of my life as a volunteer firefighter and EMT. We speak the same language. Giggle at the same insider jokes. I'll mix easily and eagerly with that crowd. But my decades serving on those departments have also taught me that what you want for a firefighter dance is a cover band that folks can drink and dance and whoop it up to—not some book writer singing his own unknown songs. By setting my ego aside and declining, I'm saving myself from having my ego crushed. And more importantly, I'm not setting up the client to be disappointed. I'll happily point them to a band better suited for the gig.

Y'gotta know your palette. My band? They're *terrific* musicians. Professionals in every sense. Me? I know a handful of chords and two rhythms. Someone once asked one of my band members if I played guitar, and without hesitation the band member replied, "Mike *has* a guitar…"

I write the songs and I sing 'em, so I'll call myself a singer/songwriter, but I know better than to call myself a *musician*.

Back to the palette: You can build a career on three colors as long as you don't labor under the illusion that you are equally capable of producing fluorescents and chartreuse.

The "Yes" of Saying "No"

Passing on Oprah gave me the nerve to pass on other tempting offers, including a recent opportunity to sell film rights for two of my books to a Hollywood production company based solely on a queasy vibe I caught in the pitch room. It wasn't easy—I gave up a modest five figures that weren't modest in proportion to our family budget—but within months the project snarled, and my instincts were validated. Had I taken the cash, my bank account would have shown a short-term bounce, but my book rights would have been forever trapped in a trash bag. Instead, I was free to shop them elsewhere, which ultimately led to a far better situation. All based on my gut. Based on feeling the project was gonna ask me to be someone I wasn't. Based on the feeling that I was being pushed past the parameters of my palette.

Oprah and Me Today

All these years later, Oprah never calls. Shoot, her *people* never call. Time is running short, and I fear it's never gonna happen. I figure you only get one chance to tell Oprah "no." But I'm forever grateful to my most famous improbable mentor for teaching me that sometimes the best way to frame the future is to take a pass in the present.

In Business Terms...

• **Align opportunities with your core values:** Pursuing every opportunity may seem advantageous, but long-term success comes from ensuring alignment with your expertise, values, and authentic brand.

• **Trust your instincts in decision-making:** Learn to recognize red flags and have the confidence to decline offers that feel misaligned, even if they appear lucrative in the short term.

• **Timing and preparation matter:** Seizing an opportunity before you are fully prepared can be counterproductive; strategic patience results in better outcomes when the right moment arrives.

PART THREE:
NURSING IT

You Have a Degree in *What?*

RECENTLY, WHILE PERFORMING IN A SMALL THEATER, I revealed that I am legally licensed to practice as a registered nurse.

The audience burst into applause.

"Ha!" I said. "You wouldn't be clapping if you were *sick*."

Y'know, because it's been *years* since I *practiced*.

Four years it took me to get that degree, and I worked as a nurse for less than two. And yet, decades after I pulled my final shift, nurses remain among my most essential, formative mentors.

What's a Nurse Got to Do with Me?

THE IMAGE IS DECADES OUT OF DATE, but to this day, mention nursing and you'll get wisecracks about shots and bedpans. But this is like saying painting is about paint. A good nurse takes your blood pressure, but also reads your eyes. Asks if you're still having that abdominal pain but also assesses your tone for more subtle signs of distress. A good nurse is driven by data and science, but also lends an ear to gut and intuition. A good nurse does their best work at the intersection of anatomy and humanity.

In short, quality nursing is predicated on human assessment. Chances are, so is your job. Or the job you *want*.

Short-term Nurse, Long-term Worth

WHEN I SHARE HOW SHORT MY NURSING CAREER WAS, folks get a look in their eye like maybe they think I turned out to be scared of blood or got caught dipping into the meds cart.

Nah. I was proud to be a nurse. Liked the work. Loved a profession where human connection was key. Did not down any Dilaudid.

What I didn't anticipate was how that nursing degree set me up for a future I didn't even see coming. Author, touring musician, public speaker, voiceover artist, playwright, screenwriter, publisher, employer, small business owner...I've drawn on my nursing background every step of the way.

Taking the Leap

I DIDN'T PLAN IT TO BE SO, but that nursing degree was my parachute. When I quit my last "real job" and leapt into full-time self-employment, I did so knowing if everything went to tatters I could pick up a good-paying nursing job in a matter of days. I didn't plan it, and I didn't know it at the time, but I was engaging in occupational cross-training. And it didn't have to be a four-year nursing degree. I've known writers with degrees or certifications or work experience in everything from landscaping to law enforcement to finance. Whether you're pursuing the arts or any other endeavor, that seemingly unrelated skill in your back pocket is both an on-ramp or an off-ramp should you need it. And it will probably hold surprising relevance to whatever tangent you pursue.

From One Thing, Another

IN THE EARLY DAYS, when I was scrapping for any writing gig I could get, I spun my experience writing encyclopedic nursing care plans and research papers into a part-time gig writing chapters for medical-legal textbooks. It wasn't the kinda thing that was gonna score me a Pulitzer, but for several years it paid the bulk of my rent. And every time I typed up another dry, over-annotated dissertation on patellar tendon ruptures, gunshot wounds, or heel bone fractures, I was *learning to write*. Like a musician playing scales or practicing fingerpicking patterns, I was laying a foundation for my craft, prepping for the time I'd be set free to riff as I pleased.

Prying Professional

Nursing also armed me with tools I used to dig for the stories that weren't on the surface.

I am pathologically shy. I hate initiating contact. As my work shifted from writing brochures and textbook chapters to writing magazine articles, I suddenly found myself thrust into a career based primarily on meeting and interviewing people I don't know. I remember staring at the phone receiver, picking it up, putting it down, picking it up, putting it down. I remember taking deep breaths before knocking on doors or approaching a subject on their turf. In many respects, writing is a sales job—and I'm not good at sales.

And so in those moments, I'd think back to the clinical wing of our nursing school, where I was taught how to walk into a small room with a disrobed stranger and ask when they last pooped. I didn't put it in those terms, of course, but when it was time for me to cold-call a trucking executive, interview a country music star on her bus, or quiz a killer in his prison cell, I didn't get all *writerly*. I just shifted to professional nurse mode.

You Don't Need
a Stethoscope to Listen

In that same little clinical room I learned not only to *ask*, but to *listen*.

"Facilitate, reflect, and clarify," my nursing instructors taught me. "Employ empathic response."

Taken to extremes, these techniques quickly become parody: "I hear you saying the steamroller ran directly over you—how does that make you *feel*?"

But when I applied them with discretion and sincerity, they were invaluable in gathering information from people for my books and articles. Turns out the interviewing tools of the nurse are eminently functional in the writing business—or *any* business. We listen best with our hearts *and* our ears.

NURSE MEETS FARM BOY

WITH ITS FOCUS ON HUMAN INTERACTION, vulnerability, and mortality, nursing was an unexpected window into the poetic, introspective parts of *me*—an otherwise stoic and knuckleheaded farm boy—that ultimately helped me connect with audiences both on and off the page. Working closely with people in their most vulnerable state drove me to contemplate my own vulnerabilities—and how many of us share these feelings. Once I recognized that connection I became better at connecting with others.

I was recently hired to interview a man for a documentary film. He was a successful businessman from a rural working-class background. Previous attempts to record his story had fallen flat largely because he was uncomfortable with the setting and process. I was brought in by a producer who knew I'd grown up farming and logging and deer hunting in the same part of the country as the businessman. I showed up for the interview in my Walmart jeans and volunteer fire department cap and shifted into a combination of nursing assessment mode and shootin' the breeze mode. While I can't claim to have established a window into the man's soul, we came away with a good batch of anecdotes and laughter and responses that sounded natural, not rote, reserved, or rehearsed.

Calling It

Nurses—and later first responders—taught me to fight on behalf of the patient's every breath. But they also taught me that in the face of failure—in this case, the ultimate failure, failing to save a life—you must gather yourself and move on to serving the next person. Framed thusly, this puts a whole new perspective on career failures. Your project got killed? Or it's dying and you don't know how to save it? Know when it's time to stop resuscitating and give life to the next thing.

Final Report

ABOVE ALL, THE REASON ALL OF MY NURSE'S TRAINING WORKED in *practice* is because our nursing instructors never let us forget that at the center of our professionalism was a vulnerable person *seeking* something. This is how I approach writing, and this is how I approach the *business* of writing. The reader wants a story. The subject wants their story told.

Told with skill.

Told with heart.

Whatever your background, whatever your story.

In Business Terms...

• **Transferable skills are invaluable:** Insights acquired in one field, even if unrelated, can provide unexpected advantages and opportunities in another by enhancing and expanding your adaptability and problem-solving skills.

• **Effective communication and human connection matter:** No matter the profession or pursuit, the ability—innate, learned, or both—to listen, empathize, and connect with people is crucial for success and growth.

• **Know when to let go and move forward:** Recognize when a project or idea isn't working and shift energy toward new opportunities.

Part Four:
Truckin'

Riding Shotgun with Stan,
Roller-skating with Snoopy

THANKS TO THE ECONOMICS OF THE TIMES, a handful of scholarships, and several side jobs (including a regular week-end gig doing the hokey-pokey on roller skates in a Snoopy costume), when I graduated from nursing school, I not only had zero student loans to pay off, I had a thousand dollars in the bank.

So I couldn't see any reason to get a job.

Instead, I went trucking with my Uncle Stan. We left rural Wisconsin with a load of cheese, hammer down for New York City. By the time we rolled home, I was hooked on the road and those who ran it.

I had grown up romanticizing Uncle Stan the trucker. He would show up at our isolated farm now and then in his big semi and give us rides, then roar off and disappear for months, running the wide-open highways and byways of America.

I now realize—as a husband, a father, and a self-employed person—that the romance of the road was counterbalanced by struggles at home, in the soul, and at the bank. But through his example, stories, and shared miles, Uncle Stan left me a flat-bed's-worth of cherished memories. Whenever I head out on my little tours, even though I'm just hauling books in a minivan, part of me imagines I'm Uncle Stan in his 18-wheeler, roarin' down the concrete superslab, pedal-to-the-metal, hood ornament aimed at some far horizon.

Uncle Stan never taught me to be a trucker—I can't run a split-shift or tarp a load—but he provided me the opportunity to look through his windshield into the trucking culture, the trucking business, and the trucking life. What I couldn't know at the time was how that view provided me priceless insights on how to survive as—of all things—a writer.

And how, in time, that window would become a door.

"Go" Beats "Show"

Back when I was first trying to be a writer, I pitched my work to the places that printed "real" writers: The big-name publishers, high-toned literary journals, and magazines like *The New Yorker, Harper's,* and *The Atlantic.*

I got nothing but *nope.*

If I was gonna pay for rent and groceries, it was clear I'd have to shoot for something other than the snooty set.

During our road trip, Uncle Stan introduced me to the trucker radio shows popular on the big 50,000-watt AM radio stations broadcasting far and wide across America after dark. A few years later while crossing North Dakota at 2 a.m. in pursuit of a magazine story in my 1989 Ford Tempo, I tuned in to *The Road Gang,* hosted out of a tiny studio in Nashville. As I listened to the trucking songs and the truckers calling in from across the nation to banter with the host and each other, it reminded me of my time with Uncle Stan. Another hundred miles down the road, I stopped at a truck stop for gas and coffee and noticed several racks of trucking magazines beside the checkout. I'd seen them around, but not being a trucker or otherwise involved in the industry, it never occurred to me that I might actually *write* for them.

I grabbed one and studied the cover.

ROAD KING, it said.

I leafed through it. There were articles about transmissions and trailers and transport laws and other things about which I had neither clue nor knowledge. But scattered throughout were personal interest stories about individual truckers, unusual trucking events, and miscellany tangentially related to trucking.

Maybe they'd publish a story about trucker radio shows, I thought.

When I got back home I typed up a pitch and mailed it.

The editor said yes, and soon I found myself in that tiny Nashville radio studio in the wee hours, watching in person as the man whose voice I'd heard coming out of my Ford Tempo radio spun tunes and fielded calls from truckers who went not by their names but their "handles"—Six-Pack, T-Trucker, King Korn, and Gatekeeper.

I wrote up the piece. The editor liked it, and I liked the check.

I pitched another story tied to my time on the road with Uncle Stan. The editor said yes again.

And again.

And again. And for the next decade, *Road King* became one of my steadiest sources of writing income. I traveled to the biggest truck show in the world. I rode with the truckers that hauled the Budweiser Clydesdales. I did stories on truckers who hauled top-secret government cargo, truckers who hauled professional motocross teams, a trucker who hauled the most expensive car in the world, and truckers who raced semi tractors up Pike's Peak.

Thanks to Uncle Stan and my willingness to shoot for the highway rather than the moon, those *Road King* assignments kept me rolling for years. They never won any fancy literary awards. They never got me invited to hang out with the cool writers. Much later, when I did ricochet through the cool kids' circle, I discovered that *Road King* rarely carried the cachet of the *Paris Review*. But if you wanna work your chops, if you wanna pay the rent, if you wanna stay in business so you can get *more* business, you need cash, not cachet. As the writer Tom McGuane once said, "I would gladly create one thousand acts of capitulation to keep my dog in Alpo." And if traveling in the company of truckers is capitulation, well, go ahead and hitch me up a load of that.

I never did break into the upper-upper echelon publications. But one of those *Road King* assignments led to a *New York Times Magazine* assignment, which led to a *GQ* assignment, which led to an *Esquire* assignment, which led to a book deal, and so on, right up to the present. Uncle Stan is gone now, but every time I stop to look in the rearview mirror, I see him back there, his trucker insights still playing out and paying out despite me never mastering the split shifter.

The Most Important Door

Uncle Stan and I had been on the road for hours when a semi roared around us in what truckers call the "hammer lane." "Third time he's passed us today," said Stan. "We'll see him again." Sure enough, when we stopped to refuel an hour later, that truck was parked in the lot. And was still there when we pulled out fifteen minutes later.

"A lot of these fellows are addicted to the truck *stop* more than truck-*ing*," said Uncle Stan. "They're always stopping to shoot the breeze or play arcade games. They get bored. Then they try to make up the time lost by driving like a wild man. Sometimes they beat me. Usually they don't." He paused a moment. Then he said, "The secret to getting ahead isn't to drive fast—it's to *keep that driver's side door shut.*"

It's the fable of the tortoise and the hare, trucker-style. So much of what we accomplish—in life, in work, in the day-to-day—is simply a result of not stopping. I've never been built for speed or splash, but good luck getting me outta low gear. I've also long claimed the secret to my middling success is being too dumb to know when to quit, and there's plenty of truth to it. Still, twenty-some books and countless essays and articles and scripts and quips and quotes and scribbles and an unexpectedly adventure-filled life later, I've come to realize: mostly I've just been working like Uncle Stan drove.

FREEDOM'S JUST ANOTHER WORD

MY TIME WITH TRUCKERS triggered my addiction to the freelance life. Both professions are fueled by freedom. Behind the wheel or behind the desk, our work allows us to observe the world on our own terms.

But my time as a writer traveling with truckers also taught me that you can run a lot of miles and see a lot of country and still develop tunnel vision, especially if you're rolling solo with just your own perceptions and perspectives. Over time I've noticed that a lot of us—truckers, farmers, freelance writers—who spend a lot of time alone develop what I call "Capital 'T' Theories." I know I do. I ruminate on them, I round up countless examples supporting them, I pet and polish them, I preach them aloud to the windshield…and then I find myself back in civilization speechifying to some thoughtful trusted friend who smiles and nods, and then says, "Well, that's not really how it works…"

We need to be challenged. Check the mirrors; leave the hammer lane for a backroad now and then. Stare straight forward and you miss the sideshows. I met more than one paranoid trucker in my day whose time on the road *shrank* their ability to learn, hope, and entertain fresh possibilities. If it didn't fit between the fog lines, it didn't fit the narrative.

Left to my own solo time and devices as I so often am, I am susceptible to these self-same blinders. Keeping this in mind, I try to leave the well-worn path now and again to immerse myself in new surroundings, fresh company, and unfamiliar experiences—even when all's I'm driving is a swivel chair.

Y'Never Know What Might Be in That Trailer

REMEMBER ALL THOSE FANCY MAGAZINES I wanted to get my stories into? Many were led by legendary editors. And filled with terrific writing. And some of those writers became my friends and mentors. To have your work reviewed and gussied up by—or share company with—those folks was an achievement in itself.

I woulda loved it.

Instead, I got stuck with the editor of *Road King*. Who—as it turned out—was an educated, erudite, well-read former investigative reporter fluent in Russian who was nonetheless happy to clamber in and out of monster trucks and chow down at a Waffle House.

Above all, he was a pro wordsmith. He consistently coached me into elevating my prose beyond what it was when I turned it in. When I signed my first book deal, I hammered away at it in a writing shack set in a horse pasture behind his house. His mentorship of me outlasted the *Road King* magazine itself and continues to this day.

I wonder sometimes where my writing career would have stalled out had I just kept clawing to get into the status magazines while assuming that writing about trucks was somehow not *writerly*, or if a man who commissioned diesel engine reviews had nothing to teach me about an artful craft. Whatever your endeavor, always remember: It's not the truck that delivers, it's the trucker. And it's nice to ride in a shiny rig, but it's what's in the trailer that pays your way.

Never Deadhead

There came a time—as a part of larger trends in the magazine world—when the *Road King* work went dry. But thanks in part to two types of truckers, I had already mapped an off-ramp. Several, as a matter of fact.

From the specialized truckers—the ones who hauled rare, high-value loads—I learned that a niche can keep you earning through the hard times. No matter the state of the economy, rich people still have fancy cars they need moved between mansions. *Road King* itself was a niche, and a productive one.

But even the richest niche can dwindle, so the more, the better. By the time *Road King* stopped hiring me, I'd cultivated other niches—country music, firefighting, regional humor essays—and had also begun repurposing my writing into a speaking, performing, and consulting career. Because of this shotgun approach, I'm not at all famous but busier than ever and currently writing my 25th book—even as the publishing industry flounders.

And then sometimes the best niche is no niche. There is a term in trucking—"LTL"—that stands for "less than load." Rather than carrying one big load of one big thing for one customer, LTL carriers haul small amounts of various products for various customers at various locations. The LTL philosophy has been a lifesaver for me. A book chapter today, a speaking engagement tomorrow, a script for a documentary next week, whatever today's customer needs, when and where they need it, I'll deliver. When you run LTL, you're filling the cracks. Satisfying asymmetrical demands. The off-kilter minutiae giant corporations and automation and algorithms aren't built to solve.

Finally, truckers taught me that the next load is never guaranteed, so it's rarely wise to sit and wait for the perfect load. In the parlance, if the wheels ain't turnin', you ain't earnin'. Better to be running half a load than no load at all—a money-losing situation truckers call "deadheading." Sometimes you take one gig to get to the next gig. Sometimes you take the job to get to the next job.

The Greasy Patch

Of all the nuggets Uncle Stan shared with me that came to serve me as a writer on the road, the one about the greasy patch is my fundamental favorite.

"See that dark patch up there?" said Uncle Stan, pointing out past his hood ornament at a blackened oval of concrete fifty yards up the road.

"Yep," I said.

"That means there's a bump ahead."

I looked at the patch again, then back at Uncle Stan.

"Tens—maybe hundreds—of thousands of vehicles are passing over that spot every day," he said. "A lot of those vehicles are leaking oil. And if a drop of that oil is ready to fall, when the wheels hit that bump, it jars loose. At interstate speeds, it'll fly several feet before it splashes down."

"So," I said, "the bump is always right before the oil patch."

"Yep," said Uncle Stan.

To this day, every time I spy a smudgy spot on the interstate I think of Uncle Stan and anticipate the bump. I am tempted to twist this into some sort of inspirational success metaphor but will settle for saying that, although I never became a trucker, I did wind up in a career where I've racked up hundreds of thousands of miles, and over those miles saved myself from slopping who knows how many gallons of gas station coffee in my lap simply because I waited to take a sip until after I was past the greasy patch.

And then I drive on, grateful for this regular reminder of my late beloved improbable mentor Uncle Stan, whose example continues to guide me in ways I never could have anticipated when I crawled up into the shotgun seat that summer after nursing school. Whatever your pursuit, your most enduring mentors may be the ones whose lessons are allegorical rather than literal. In my case, if it wasn't for my truckin' uncle, I might very well still be sittin' here grinding my gears.

In Business Terms...

- **Adaptability and niche focus lead to longevity:** Remain open and alert to new perspectives that challenge assumptions, identify specialized niches, and diversify your skills to remain relevant in a shifting environment.

- **Don't confuse image with success:** Prestige is fleeting; sustainable and rewarding careers are built through effort, real-world experience, and seizing available opportunities.

- **Stay in motion:** Lasting success is predicated less on speed than momentum.

PART FIVE:
EVERYTHING'S AN EMERGENCY

WHERE'S THE LADDER?

IT WAS A PEACEFUL, SUNNY DAY.

Then my fire department pager went off.

Unconscious male, said the dispatcher. *Wife reports he fell off a ladder in the garage and hit his head.*

I radioed in and headed for the address. Following a few miles of winding country road, I spotted a matching number on the mailbox and accelerated up a smooth asphalt driveway curling uphill through tall pines. The lawn was neat, the house well kept, and through the open garage door I could see the unconscious man lying on a clean concrete floor.

I knelt at his head and immediately spotted a hemorrhaging head wound. A woman appeared, obviously shaken.

"Are you his wife?" I asked.

She nodded.

I was about to continue when I noticed something.

There was no ladder.

Rule Number One

My earliest emergency medical service mentor was an EMT instructor named Jim. The first rule Jim taught us was *never enter a scene until you know it is secure*.

That is to say, don't be so intent on being a hero that you run headlong into an unstable or dangerous situation and destabilize it even more by becoming endangered yourself. Suddenly your fellow rescuers are dealing with *two* victims.

That day in the garage, I didn't know it—and I certainly didn't spot it early enough—but the scene was *not* secure.

"We were told he fell off a ladder," I said to the man's wife.

She shot a nervous glance at the house and then back to me.

"My son did this," she said.

My heart did a flip-flop.

"Where is your son?"

"In there," she said, nodding toward the house.

"Is he a threat to us?" I asked. "Is he armed?"

"I don't know," said the wife. "There are guns in there."

My guts went chill. Just then a second first responder arrived. I told him to back off to the perimeter, keep his eye on the house, and radio the sheriff's department. I had already started to treat the patient, so I couldn't leave him. I sweated it out, one eye on the patient and one eye on the house, my ears straining for the sound of squad cars.

THE SCENE SURVEY

IN LAW ENFORCEMENT, FIREFIGHTING, AND EMS, every call begins with a "scene survey." Just as Jim taught us, before you can secure the scene, you must *survey* the scene. Assess it. Scan for anomalies. For what doesn't add up. For what doesn't match.

In other words, look before you leap.

Safety is the primary driver, but once we transitioned from surveying the scene to surveying the patient, the concept took on wider relevance. As both a nurse and an EMT, I was warned against the tunnel vision that could distract me from the real problem. The grotesquely distorted leg of the guy who crashed his motorcycle? Important, and we'll get around to it, but first we scan head-to-toe (no matter where the toe might be at the moment) so we don't miss the slight deviation in his trachea or the bruise behind his ear that might be far more life-threatening.

Let's say you suspect the motorcyclist has an internal injury: before you palpate the abdomen or pull out your stethoscope and listen to the abdomen, you *survey* at the abdomen. *Look* at it before you touch it.

There are the obvious reasons—you're scanning for any obvious injury or deformity—but less obviously, if you start by touching the abdomen, the patient may engage in *guarding*, in which they tense their stomach muscles. This can obscure an underlying distension or lump or other problem. It also causes pain, which can compromise the accuracy of the rest of the assessment by affecting the patient's ability to describe how they were feeling *before* you jabbed their throbbing appendix.

This approach has served me well outside the world of emergencies. I was once assigned to write a story about two combat-wounded veterans attempting to summit Mt. Rainier. For the same reason we don't just come roaring in and jab the abdomen, I didn't attempt to interview either man ahead of time. Theirs were powerfully personal stories of war and death and loss; the last thing they needed was some stranger grilling them on a phone call. The far more respectful and effective way to reach the heart of their stories was simply to show up and climb beside them. To let their powerful stories emerge organically rather than try to awkwardly extract them.

And that's exactly what happened. We met at the base of the mountain, did our hellos, and started climbing. Started with all the standard pleasantries and breeze-shooting. Spent the day talking about everything but the heavy stuff. Did a little tentative joking around. Got to know each other as individuals rather than interviewer and subjects. And then, a couple days in, halfway up the mountain and exhausted, the two soldiers sat down while the guides made camp and started telling *each other* their stories. I didn't have to do a thing but shut up and get it down. The result was one of the most powerful pieces of writing I've ever been privileged to share*—and all because I held back rather than rushed in.

In life and business, the "first mover" advantage can be the difference between winning or losing. You don't want to dither. But sometimes a little pause upon arrival to look things over is equally important.

It's tough to take that moment. To pause. To maintain a holding pattern when every fiber of your being wants to drop the nose and dive. We are wired to charge forward, when in fact waiting and watching can be a critical element of success. So whether I'm responding to an emergency call or a simple opportunity I try to remember: Don't confuse "first mover" advantage with "first fatality" *dis*advantage.

* This story appears in the "Men Among Men" section of my book *Danger: Man Working* under the title "Shock and Awe."

Solve for the Truth

Ultimately, under guard of law enforcement, we got the unconscious man to the ambulance and on his way to the hospital. I never did see the son. But I drove home with a tremor in my gut at how badly things could have gone. I had broken a cardinal rule—I entered a scene before ensuring it was safe. And this happened because I hadn't questioned what I had been told—I simply assumed it to be true.

What I finally asked—but should have asked much sooner—is, what *really* happened here?

When I went on my first "official" book tour in the early 2000s, I thought that the key was to get great turnout at book signings. This was daunting, as I was an unknown midwestern writer. But the publisher did a terrific job of promotion, and despite my rookie status, when I hit big cities, I'd be on morning television shows, I'd do numerous radio interviews, I'd be in the book sections of the big newspapers, there'd be an article in the local alt-weekly, and so on.

As a result, many of my book signings were far better attended than I had any right to expect. But even if there were more empty chairs than occupied, sales of my book in that city bumped upward for a good ten days surrounding my visit.

So what was *really* happening here?

It turned out that other than its effect on my ego, the number of people in the seats for a reading was far less important than the number of people who heard me on the radio, saw me on television, or read about me in the paper. From that first tour forward, I always loved a good turnout and did whatever I could to ensure one, but I also never forgot the *real* purpose of a book tour: to leverage the halo of attention *surrounding* the individual events.

Flash forward twenty years. I'm still relatively unknown but have sold a few hundred thousand books and still benefit from the promotions arm of a major publisher. Except now if I go to Seattle, I'm lucky to get one or two interviews. Social media has displaced legacy media. The newspaper book sections are gone. Broadly speaking, book publishing is in a state of disruption and decline. If the publisher sends me on tour, the budget is a shadow of what it once was, and that two-week sales bump is more of a sales blip.

Authors love to complain about book tours, but very few of those authors have ever had to make a living logging. I'm pretty sure most authors covet book tours (I know I do) because being able to say "I'm on *book tour*" supports the *image* we covet. It also represents something we worked hard for. And in the salad days, my publisher not only covered my food and travel expenses, they put me up in a Seattle hotel in which every room had its own goldfish.

So I'd love to just keep doing book tours the way we used to do them. But after my most recent experience, I realized it was once again time to ask: "What is *really* happening here?" And what was *really* happening was that traditional touring (and to an extent, even traditional publishing) weren't working for me the way they used to.

I didn't mourn; I switched up. Continued writing for major publishers. Continued gratefully accepting and amplifying whatever support they were willing to provide. But I also started self-publishing when it made more sense (I sell far fewer books but make more money faster). I started focusing less on *book* tours and more on *paying* tours where I get a speaking fee and my contract includes a rider ensuring I am allowed to sell my books before and after the event.

It's not as romantic as the book tours of yore.

No more hotel room goldfish.

But in emergency rescue or book touring or whatever your endeavor, being willing to accept that the scene has changed or isn't what you thought it was may be the key to survival.

QUESTION AUTHORITY

A MAN FLIPPED HIS CAR AT 3 A.M. IN A BLIZZARD and my partner Jacques and I were the only rescue crew available. The driver was drunk and cursing as we immobilized his neck with a collar and strapped and buckled his upper torso into a specialized extrication device. We were being pelted by wind and sleet and cuss words, but we persevered, having been drilled and drilled on this very specific procedure and equipment and warned that to divert from it was to risk paralyzing the patient for life. Finally we were set to pull the man free—at which point we discovered the car had been crushed in such a way that there was no way he could be removed while wrapped in all that mandated equipment. He simply wouldn't fit through the available window, and there was no extrication equipment or "jaws of life" inbound any time soon.

The next thing I knew, Jacques was popping snaps and buckles and stripping the equipment away—a big no-no, per standard operating procedures. Then he grabbed a blanket and spun it into a roll, at which point I realized he was about to deploy a rapid-extrication technique called a "horse collar." Looping the rolled blanket around the man's neck and passing the free ends beneath the man's armpits, Jacques grabbed the ends, dragged the man (still cussing) out, and ten minutes later we deposited him into a warm hospital bed. I figured we'd be sued into oblivion, but the man's spine was fine. Most importantly, given the conditions and circumstances, Jacques had made the right call.

I included the horse collar story in my first truly successful book, *Population 485*, which centered on serving on a volunteer fire and rescue service with my neighbors. For both the hardcover and paperback I tried to get my publisher to supplement my standard book tour by sending me to emergency medical and firefighting conventions. They always demurred, and in more than one instance came right out and said EMTs and firefighters weren't a good book-buying demographic.

I can understand the publisher's position—to a point. If you want to sell books, you want to get your author in front of readers. Where do readers go? Bookstores, of course. And in my case, independent bookstores, the heroes of my existence.

But what if your author is in front of a sterile but gigantic conference room packed with paramedics, EMTs, firefighters, and other first responders? And what if not a single person in that room came to the conference planning to buy a book— let alone *read* one—but then heard someone who speaks their language and tells their story in a way they can relate to? Someone who can bring them to laughter and tears because they see themselves in the story?

And then what if, in the glow of that moment, the author moves from the microphone to a table (strategically positioned beside the exit) stacked with copies of that very book—and it's the only book in the room?

I can tell you exactly what happens, because when it became clear the publisher wasn't going to act on my suggestion, I started pitching myself to these conventions. Twenty years, hundreds of speaking engagements, and tens of thousands of books later, I'm still doing it. Only now it's not just that one book; it's all my books. And a few T-shirts, posters, and can koozies to boot. And this "non-literary" crowd has not only bought thousands of copies of *Population 485*, but many have also bought every book I've published since. This isn't a brag. This isn't me dismissing the publishers and booksellers to whom I owe vast swaths of my career. It's just that sometimes the main way isn't the only way. The usual target isn't the only target. This isn't a zero-sum game. It's *additive*.

And here's the bonus: Book sales and business aside, I enjoy hanging out and swapping stories with folks in the rescue world. We speak the same language. We've shared the same adrenaline and heartbreak. We know what it's like to work under adverse conditions and how sometimes emergency rescue is like golf: You gotta play it where it lies. If your patient is upside down in a ditch or jammed in a crushed car, you might have to accept that usual ways ain't gonna do it, no matter how long you've been doing it or how it worked in the past. And sometimes the obvious ways aren't always the most productive. You might have to toss out standard operating procedures, roll up that blanket and drag things to a better place.

In Business Terms...

- **Assess before acting:** Always question the obvious.

- **Adapt to changing realities:** Honor tradition when appropriate and relevant but look beyond it to recognize shifts and adjust strategies accordingly; to thrive you must first survive.

- **Test the rules:** Challenge assumptions and explore unconventional approaches.

PART SIX:
THE QUESTION NO ONE IS ASKING

What Not to Do

Sometimes your improbable mentors remain name-less. You don't interact, they don't take you under their wing, you don't confab, you simply learn by watching what they do.

And if you watch carefully, you'll notice what they *don't* do.

And that's your opening.

Your shot at the happy tangent.

ALWAYS BE CLOSING

ONCE UPON A TIME I was standing at the end of a long line in a humid press tent waiting to interview country music superstars Brooks & Dunn. I was working as a stringer for *Country Weekly*, a national music magazine, meaning I was hired to attend a local country music festival, interview as many performers as possible, and churn out short reports.

The publication armed me with boilerplate interview questions and a press pass. After that I was on my own. Often I was allowed only a minute or two for the interview, so I'd have to hustle through my questions. Fortunately, we weren't talking in-depth Pulitzer stuff. A couple of quotes, a few lines of description, and on to the next act.

On average, I did five or six of these interviews a day. As an unknown freelance stringer writing for a print publication, I was nearly always last in line after the television people, the local radio personalities, and various full-time reporters. I was the outsider, the non-journalist still learning the trade. I watched how the folks ahead of me operated and quickly determined the procedure was generally the same:

REPORTER: "So what do you think of the Country Blast music festival?"

COUNTRY STAR: "We LOVE the Country Blast music

festival. And we just want to thank the fans. It's the *fans* that make it a blast."

REPORTER: "How is the tour going?"

COUNTRY STAR: "The tour has been amazing. And we just want to thank the fans for that. It's the *fans* that make the tour amazing."

REPORTER: "How is the new album doing?"

COUNTRY STAR: "The new album is doing amazing. And we just want to thank the fans for their support. It's the *fans* that buy the albums."

REPORTER: "How about the new single?"

COUNTRY STAR: "The new single is doing great. And that's because of the fans."

Both parties had a job to do, and they were doing it. The performers stuck to the "thank the fans" script but were generally sincere. Sincerity and good business aren't necessarily mutually exclusive.

It was literally my *job*—if I wanted to *keep* my job—to ask the same questions. Even though I'd heard the answers six times already.

There was also no hiding the rote nature of the exercise. Often by the time I was allowed my five questions, I could see the entertainer's eyes glazing.

So, having had time to observe, I came up with a plan.

A selfish plan. A *tangent*.

And it paid off. For years.

Going Off Script

I BEGAN THE INTERVIEW LIKE EVERY INTERVIEWER PRECED-
ING ME.

"So, what do you think of the Country Blast festival?"

You know the rest.

But once I asked the questions *Country Weekly* wanted me
to ask, I asked one of my own.

I'd been thinking on it. Trying to come up with one they
didn't hear day after day. One that might nudge them off
script. One every entertainer could answer but hadn't likely
had to answer before.

Then one day I was on the sidewalk when a shiny tour bus
pulled away from a downtown hotel and made its way toward
the festival grounds. Everyone (including me) turned their
heads for a look. The question foremost in our minds was
who's on the bus?

And as I stared at that gleaming chromed-out land yacht, a
much better question hit me. And the next time I got through
my list of *Country Weekly* questions with a worn-out superstar, I asked one of my own:

"What can you tell me about your bus driver?"

And oh man, the floodgates opened. From the burnished
legends to the fresh-faced newcomers, each performer lit up at

the chance to talk about someone other than themselves. The stories just *rolled* out. "Well c'mon and *meet* 'im!" said Charlie Daniels, referring to his driver Dean Tubb (son of Ernest), and minutes later I was in a recliner on Mr. Daniels' bus chatting while Mrs. Daniels cooked supper on the stove. "Oh, lemme *tell ya* about ol' Hoot Gibson!" said Mark Miller, the lead singer of Sawyer Brown, and there followed a chorus of legendary tales. When I finally got my chance to interview Vince Gill, it was nearly 10 pm, and he was leaning against a tent pole, visibly weary. "Tell me about your bus driver," I said, and twenty minutes later he was still talking, happy and animated as he flowed from anecdote to anecdote.

I wound up harvesting pages of rich material. But even more importantly for my writing career, I made contacts and was given access and insights yielding up tangents leading to story after story somehow tied to country music bus drivers. I worked off this goldmine for years, pitching and placing stories about a trucker who hauled a section of Reba McEntire's stage on tour; a group of drivers who used their fancy buses to take underprivileged kids shopping at Christmas; a first-person piece in which Discovery Channel sent me out on tour with Marty Stuart and his band. Even seemingly unrelated stories I did years later—traveling with truckers on the professional motocross circuit, for example—could be traced back to unlikely tangents sprung from my time as a stringer standing last in line.

Years later, I'd meet the author and speaker Andy Andrews, and he'd summarize my experience in a single statement: *The most critical question we can ask is the question no one is asking.**

To this day I'm grateful to the professionals in line ahead of me who showed me the ropes. Taught me how to ask the questions I needed to ask—all the while giving me time to come up with one of my own. The one no one was asking. The one that triggered a multitude of tangents. The one that led me to tell (and sell) stories no one had asked me for. The one that kept me in business because I went one question beyond business as usual.

*Andy expands on the concept of the question no one is asking in his book *The Bottom of the Pool.*

In Business Terms...

• **Observe and innovate:** Pay close attention to norms, then identify gaps or overlooked perspectives where you can offer something fresh and valuable.

• **Shift your perspective:** Prospect for actionable insights by—literally and figuratively—observing subjects or processes from atypical angles.

• **Leverage tangents for growth:** A single unconventional idea or insight can open doors to long-term opportunities, networks, and business expansion far beyond your original scope.

PART SEVEN:
DO YOU SMELL SMOKE?

Mentors in Flames

Many of the most meaningful experiences of my life have taken place beneath a fire helmet. I loved fighting fires. Loved packing up and crawling into a flaming trailer house. Loved fighting the buck of the hose while trying to extinguish a factory fire while encased head-to-toe in ice. Loved the smoky skirmish of battling a wildland fire. And to this day I cherish what I learned from the men and women who responded and fought beside me.

Also, the lights and sirens were a blast.

But the finest lessons my firefighting mentors taught me had less to do with heroic hoo-hah than solid decision making.

Caution Doesn't Equal Cowardice

FIREFIGHTING CAN BLAST THROUGH PRETENSE LIKE A BLOWTORCH THROUGH BUTTER. The difference between bravery and bravado can be judged by various measures, one of them being 525°F, the temperature at which your face shield melts and drips to the floor, followed milliseconds later by your face.

There are also less fatal gauges. On one occasion, my partner and I were cautiously mopping up the tail end of a fire on the second floor of a house when a firefighter from another department got frustrated with our refusal to move forward. We told him we feared the floor had been weakened by the fire. Hero Boy grabbed an ax, charged past us, and fell straight through the floorboards, saved only by the fact that he was straddling a stringer. He took a solid shot to the nuts, which was nice. It was a treat to watch him teeter.

My theory is, if a guy has a No Fear sticker or the equivalent on his helmet, he's welcome to the front of the hose—the only danger being he may trample you on the way out when everything goes south and his courage melts as quick as his stickers.

I've mentioned the "first mover" advantage earlier in this book, and no doubt there are times by refusing to jump in

I have missed out. But I remember far more times when I felt the itch to charge ahead—be it on the latest social media platform, or some new investment strategy or hot stock, or a bestselling book trend—and held back only to watch from the sidelines as it all crashed and burned, or, more likely, melted slowly into yesterday's news.

Exit Strategies Are Essential

The pumper operator and I were watching from across the street as the chief and a dozen firefighters clustered near the doorway of a burning warehouse, preparing to attack. Suddenly, a vicious whistling erupted from within the building, the volume and pitch spiraling louder and louder by the second. The way everybody came peeling out of there, it was like someone had kicked an anthill. I jumped behind a tree. Eventually, the noise whistled down to nothing (it turned out to be air escaping from a pressurized container), but I still chuckle when I think of how unabashedly we bailed.

Firefighters are trained to attack but prepared to retreat. We keep a hand or a knee in constant contact with the hose while we're inside a structure. Like Tom Sawyer's string strung through a cavern, it's your way out should things go bad. When it comes to firefighting, buying real estate, or salvaging a relationship, positive thinking has its place, but in any of these endeavors, there are advantages to assuming the worst and preplanning your escape.

A United States Marine Corps veteran mentor of mine—who didn't fight fire but survived many a firefight—planted this way of thinking in me years ago. While serving as a helicopter pilot in Vietnam he was shot down twice and was twice injured in ground combat, collecting a pair of Purple Hearts. Despite these brushes with death, he volunteered to fly fighter jet sorties. When someone remarked on how brave and noble he was to take on this extra duty, he grinned and said, "Nah, I just liked being in an aircraft that could retreat at 600 miles per hour."

When in Doubt, Crawl

ANY BASIC FIRE SAFETY BROCHURE can tell you how to act if you are caught inside a burning building (remain calm, stay low, do not open a warm door, etc.), but there are other firefighter tricks that can raise your odds of rescue. I was third man in on an interior attack of an active house fire when the lead man tumbled face-first into a basement full of flames. Had he been walking upright, he would have disappeared feet-first into the inferno. Instead, he was on all fours, which extended his body and gave him just enough time to delay his fall so that the number two man could hoist him out by his legs.

While I have employed this technique many times as a firefighter, I have also deployed it in my career through its much less dramatic figurative equivalent: low overhead. As much as I talk about making the leap into my self-employed freelance life, I have more frequently survived in the long term less by leaping than by slowly merging and not getting in over my head. I will never know if this approach has kept me from becoming a filthy rich superstar. But I do know it has allowed me to amortize risk and accrete solid success one layer at a time and has led me to a place of happiness and relative security. And I suspect for someone brighter than I, it is scalable.

Some people shoot for the stars. Some of us crawl, so there ain't so far to fall.

If You Screw It Up,
Don't Cover It Up

Back in the day, we reserved an entire segment of our annual banquet for bonehead awards. Once, the chief completely missed the truck bay and backed the rapid-attack truck smack into the wall. He toyed with the idea of keeping the whole thing on the down-low, until someone saw the bumper-wide crease in the steel siding. At the banquet, our beefiest firefighter dressed in drag and sang him the "Back It Up Blues."

Another year, I got an award for leaving a midnight accident scene and driving halfway home before realizing I was at the wheel of another firefighter's car. I got busted by a bunch of my guffawing comrades when I tried to sneak through the roadblock to make the trade back.

More seriously, once a month, we'd review our calls and speak frankly about what we did wrong and what we could have done better. We had to be willing to set aside our egos and not worry about tromping on others'. It didn't always work—we're humans with pride, false and otherwise—but those bonehead awards helped. For all their goof-off, back-slapping fun, they fostered a spirit of openness in which it was okay to admit screwups.

I've tried to carry this spirit into my non-firefighting work. My performing career has been extremely regional. I can sell out a 400-seat theater in southern Wisconsin but struggle to sell 20 tickets in a joint across the Minnesota border. I shared this with someone recently, and they tried to reassure me that surely it wasn't so.

But it *is* so. I've seen the numbers.

If I do a live event and ticket sales are disappointing, I am disappointed too. But rather than dwell on it, my manager and I explore the possible reasons. Was it me? Was it the venue? Was it the calendar? Ultimately, we determine whether to tweak the approach and give it another go or move on. But we don't ignore it.

I'm also fortunate in that our little business travels light. We're not rakin' it in, but neither are we indebted or desperate. Our number one goal is not to get bigger, just better. And I've got low emotional overhead because even if I never sold another book or ticket, the rural farm kid in me would look back in wonder at all I was allowed.

But until I can't, I'm keepin' at it. And that includes acting like a firefighter. Reviewing every call. Celebrating the successful ones but also assessing and accepting accountability for the ones that weren't so stellar.

I've had a lot of practice. A while back we got paged out on a trauma call, and I jumped into the ambulance and roared out of the garage without unplugging the electrical charger.

When the call was over, I left the following note on the whiteboard:

Yes, someone took off in Unit 245 without unplugging the landline.

No, the pigtail did not detach.

Yes, the main cord ripped itself out by the roots about 30 feet up.

No, Mike Perry would really rather not discuss it.

But by now you know: Of course we did.

In Business Terms…

• **Calculated caution wins:** True success isn't about reckless bravery but about assessing risks wisely, knowing when to move forward, and when to hold back to avoid costly failures.

• **Always have an exit strategy:** Whether in firefighting or business, planning for contingencies and being prepared to pivot can be the difference between survival and failure.

• **Own your mistakes and learn from them:** Transparency, accountability, and the ability to analyze missteps without ego create a culture of improvement and long-term success.

PART EIGHT:
NAMING NAMES

The Roundup

This deep into my thicket of tangents, I have more improbable mentors than one little book can contain. I suspect it is the same for you. For this the penultimate section, I offer a brief roundup of just a few of these folks and the nuggets of wisdom they left me to carry in my pocket right up to this very moment.

WILLIE WILLIAMS

MY RANCH BOSS IN WYOMING FOR FIVE YEARS and one of my most formative mentors. Best piece of advice he ever gave me? I was pursuing a girl who was not only out of my league but known for leading naïve young country boys down the path of iniquity. One day when Willie and I were doing some ironwork in the shop, I mentioned my romantic twinges for this young lady. Willie flipped his welding helmet up, fixed me with a death stare, and in a booming voice, said, "Son, *RUN LIKE YOU WAS BEIN' SHOT AT!*"

And then he went back to welding.

And I did not go back to that girl. It's likely I saved myself some trouble and her some boredom.

Just this moment it occurs to me Willie never specified whether he meant run *away* or run *toward*…but based on his gaze and tone I believe my instincts were right, and to this day, when I find myself in a situation where my gut or my heart are wavering, I remember: Persistence isn't always your pal; sometimes it's cut and run that saves your buns.

G. Preston Williams
the Third

THE FATHER OF WILLIE AND MY ORIGINAL WYOMING BOSS. We called him Pres, pronounced *press*. Every summer for decades, Pres hired hay crews. Rather than seasoned hands, he preferred high schoolers or even college kids from the city. His explanation was that it was easier to teach the greenhorns than some older person who thinks they know better.

I was sixteen when I hired on. One rainy day when we couldn't make hay, Pres scattered us around the ranch and assigned us each a different task: fixing fence, painting his wife's kitchen, sharpening sickles. I was dispatched to build corral panels from lodgepole pine. I made good progress but was frustrated by having to arrange and nail the poles myself. When Pres stopped by and asked how things were going, I told him I could crank out more panels if he'd send one or two of the other hands to help me. It seemed he hadn't heard me, so I asked a second time. Squaring up and looking out beneath the brim of his Stetson, he said, "Son, I know you *think* it'll be faster, but if there's one thing I've learned runnin' this place, it's this: One boy is a help…two boys is half-a-help…and three boys ain't *no help at all*."

I still think we coulda added a couple extra panels to the stack if he'd'a given me a helper that day. But more than once in the years since as a bandleader and boss and event organizer I've drawn on the Pres approach: sometimes the best way to get things done is to send everyone to their own corner and let 'em do what they do.

Mrs. Rehrauer, Mrs. Beier, Miss Grant

In retrospect these three women seem to be very probable mentors, but at the time, the relevance of their influence was utterly unforeseen.

Mrs. Rehrauer was my seventh-grade English teacher. I was a well-read but tractor-driving, football-playing, class-clowning knucklehead. One day we showed up to class expecting to circle verbs and underline nouns, and instead Mrs. Rehrauer directed our attention to a black-and-white photo of an abandoned farmhouse she had taped to the blackboard and said, "Your assignment today is to study that photo and write whatever comes to mind."

Unused to such an open-ended assignment, I spent the first several minutes dithering, not sure how to start. But then I started writing. Spinning a story out of my imagination and onto the page. Something along the lines of, "I am an old man returned to the house of my childhood. Yonder the clover fields of my youth…."

It was pretty bad.

But it also gave me a thrill. The same thrill I felt when I was heading out to go deer hunting or suiting up for a football game. A thrill I never expected to feel in English class.

I handed it in, and nothing much changed. By the time I got to football practice that afternoon I was the same old knucklehead. Years passed. I went to college for a nursing degree. Somewhere in there I was required to take a creative writing course.

And with our first assignment, there was that thrill again, shooting me right back to Mrs. Rehrauer's room. Wait a minute, I thought. Maybe this is what I wanna do. From that moment on, even as I completed my degree and hired on as a nurse, I was setting my sails for the day I could write every day—and thanks to the spark struck by Mrs. Rehrauer, I got there.

Mrs. Beier was my high school English teacher. I disrupted and ran my mouth in her class so often that when she died twenty-five years later, I wrote a letter of apology to her family. As a result, I can't say Mrs. Beier taught me a lot about writing, but she always kept stacks of *New Yorker* magazines in her room, and between skipping class and pulling disruptive stunts, I went through them, page by page, reading all the cartoons. Those cartoons were different than the ones in our small-town newspaper. They introduced me to concepts like art and abstraction and irony and absurdity and observational humor and implied a whole world beyond my smug teenaged literalism. Those cartoons percolated in my head for years and were one of innumerable signposts that pointed me down the endless forking paths that have left my life enriched by reading and writing every day.

And finally, Miss Grant. Senior year in high school. I took her class for all the wrong reasons. Figured I was sneaking a low-effort credit. Rather than treat me like the adolescent know-it-all I was, Miss Grant taught me a skill I have used nearly every day for the past 30 years as a means of employment, of feeding my kids, and of unanticipated adventure, joy, and fulfillment.

Miss Grant taught me how to type.

CLYDE STUBBLEFIELD

CLYDE STUBBLEFIELD WAS JAMES BROWN'S LONGTIME DRUMMER. His "Funky Drummer" performance is one of the most sampled music tracks in history, and his drumsticks are in the Rock & Roll Hall of Fame. Clyde Stubblefield and I shared little in the way of musical talent, but as longtime Wisconsin residents, we crossed paths now and then. And although Clyde was originally from the South, his time up north left him intimately familiar with the dangers and discomforts of bitter cold.

So it came to be I found myself backstage with Mr. Stubblefield discussing the difficulties of making a living as a self-employed artist—in particular how often we are asked to do something for free because "it will be good exposure."

"Young man," said Mr. Stubblefield, bringing his face in close to mine, "Never forget: You can *die* from exposure!"

In short: *Get paid.*

ANDY ANDREWS

AUTHOR, COMEDIAN, AND MOTIVATIONAL SPEAKER ANDY ANDREWS has mentored me in multiple respects—including fishing. Recently while adrift in the Gulf of Mexico with time to kill courtesy of a dead boat motor, we had a wide-ranging conversation. At some point, I mentioned how reading two biographies of the French philosopher and playwright Voltaire helped me navigate a tough mental patch.

"Oh!" said Andy, nodding vigorously. "I love to read biographies of dead people because the verdict is in! You can see their mistakes and successes and weigh them against the final result."

Whatever the trouble or conundrum—business or personal—Andy and I agree: sometimes it's best to curl up with a good book and let the dead people speak.

AL ROSS

AL WAS A REGIONAL RADIO PERSONALITY, SOMETIMES BUSINESS PARTNER, AND FRIEND. He had a classic radio voice—what Al referred to as his "velvet pipes." We spent countless hours in studios together while he recorded the voice-overs and ad copy we co-wrote. He taught me that no two microphones are the same and to listen carefully for the "gain" on a mic—in simplest terms, how the sound changes depending on how close your mouth is as you speak. As a result, whenever I have a speaking engagement, I try to stand in the back of the room or in the wings and listen to the preceding speaker...or at the very least listen to the person doing my introduction. Time and time again I watch speakers "swallow" the mic and cause distortion or speak from too far away, not realizing their voice isn't transmitting through the speakers. You can also use the range and sensitivity of the gain to add dynamics to your presentation—leaning in closer to the mic to hit a punchline, for example. Tiny things, but they contribute to a markedly better audience experience. By the time I take the stage, I usually have a good sense of these things, and every single time I step up to speak, I think of Al, my microphone mentor.

Bob Carr

Long before I knew what I wanted to do with my life, I had this hazy idea that I should get better at presenting myself in public (like many speakers and performers, in day-to-day circumstances I am an awkwardly shy stumblebum), so I started doing plays with a local community theater company. The mentors and lessons I carry from those times deserve their own book, but one mentor stands out for one fundamentally useful lesson.

Our productions took place in a lovely but cavernous old theater known for swallowing sound. If you didn't learn to project your voice, the audience would hear a muffled nothing. During our final dress rehearsals, Bob would disappear into the shadowy far reaches of the old joint, and as you delivered your lines a voice would emanate from the darkness, declaring (in the most theatrical of tones), "Pro-*JEH*-ECT!"

In the early days, it wasn't uncommon for me to arrive at a speaking engagement only to find an ancient static-riddled microphone, a blown speaker, or no sound system at all. Every time, I'd imagine Bob at the back of the room, take a deep breath (sometimes climbing up atop a chair or table, and once, a fence post), and pro-*JEH*-ECT.

These days, thanks to my manager, I'm happy to say the average sound situation is much improved—but just last week, when the microphone failed mid-speech at an outdoor event, I simply stepped to the front of the stage and switched to "Pro-*JEH*-ECT!" mode while the sound man re-rigged the gear.

That hint of a grin on my face? That was me smiling at the memory of Bob.

Farmer Dad
and the Old-timers

My father* was a city kid who took up farming in the late 1960s. The old-timers who mentored him recommended if he wanted to survive farming he should milk cows year 'round, log in the winter, and keep a flock of sheep. Their philosophy being: the milk check was your main source of income; logging was the perfect winter pursuit because it was easier to skid logs over frozen ground, you couldn't work in the fields anyway, and the lumber brought in extra cash; and, on a good year the money you made selling lambs and wool covered the property taxes. This old-fashioned philosophy (and his stubborn refusal to take on debt) helped my father survive as other small farms disappeared or were absorbed by the "get big or get out" trends that still rule today. And above all it meant that he got to make a living doing something he loved. Today he's in his 80s and still happily at it.

Although my father and the old-timers never used the phrase, what they were working here was what your corporate types refer to as "multiple revenue streams." And consciously or not, I followed their example to survive as a writer. Rather than put all my effort into just one magazine or riding a one-off bestselling book, I branched out into speaking. Freelance editing. Voice-over work. Podcasting. Consulting. With the soft hands of a writer but the determination of a farmer, I've been able to ride the flips and flops, the wins and whoopsies, indeed the implosion of entire industries—and never had to hit pause on the thing I love most: writing. And just like Dad, I am still happily at it.

*You'd think there might be more about Dad in this book, but he wasn't an improbable mentor, he was my number one mentor. I've written more elsewhere about his lasting influence, most of all in the book *Coop*.

BILLY KRAUSE

BILLY WAS THE FIRST MUSICIAN TO EVER TAKE MY SONG-
WRITING SERIOUSLY and encourage me to play those songs
in public. By then I was comfortable on stage as a speaker and
humorist, but I was petrified at the idea of singing and playing
guitar for a live audience. In particular, I worried about playing the wrong chord or forgetting lyrics during a live show. If
I'm giving a speech or reading a poem or an essay and make
a mistake, I can just back up and start over. It ain't pretty, but
it's an option.

But a song requires uninterrupted forward motion. Flub a
word or a chord, and the band plays past you. You gotta figure out how to catch up. To recover on the fly. Meanwhile, the
band isn't playing a D chord anymore.

I remember the first time I admitted my fear of flubs to Billy.
We were just about to step onstage. Smiling like a Zen master,
he said, "Just keep strummin' and smilin'—they'll never know."

And he was right. In the years since that moment, I have
lost count of how many times I've gotten off-track, be it in a
song or some other circumstance, and rather than panic and
shut it all down, I just—sometimes literally and sometimes figuratively—kept strummin' and smilin,' nobody noticed, and
we came out the other side just fine.

ANONYMOUS ROADIE

ONCE WHILE ON TOUR WITH A COUNTRY MUSIC BAND I was profiling I found myself hungrily eyeing a table of food backstage at an amphitheater in Petaluma, California. The food was nothing fancy, mostly what a musician friend of mine once referred to as "sweaty meats and cheeses," but I was in the odd position of being *with* the band but not *of* the band, so I wasn't sure I should partake.

A man appeared at my elbow. A roadie, clad in the standard bandana, black heavy metal T-shirt, and cargo shorts. Probably in his 50s. Maybe his sixties. Hard to tell. Had some miles on him. He looked at me, looked at the food, then looked at me again.

"Go ahead, man."

"I don't know if I should…I'm not really—"

He shook his head and smiled. "Yer new, aren't ya? You live on the road, there's two rules: When you see food, *eat it*. When you get ten minutes, *sleep*."

I got myself a plate. And then a nap.

Part Nine
The Most Improbable Mentor
Move of All

Make Your Own Music,
Make Your Own Mark

ONCE UPON A TIME, A YOUNG MUSICIAN—having observed me making my middling way as a freelance writer and author—approached me for advice on how to make it as an independent artist. I was certainly no big shot, but I was a decade in to making a living at it and had learned a thing or two, so I advised him to the best of my ability.

Over time the musician's career grew, but eventually it plateaued short of what he hoped, and he began casting about for a new direction. He'd call me a lot during these times, sometimes at 2 a.m., and we'd talk about what it took to survive, and what he might try, and what I'd learned over time that might be relevant to his situation. Then one night he called and said that after much trepidation and consideration he had decided to radically rethink his sound, but he was hesitant because it would require reconfiguring or sacrificing most of what he'd built to that point, including his band, which included some dear and longtime friends.

I knew the band. They were my friends too. I suspected there would be hurt feelings and maybe hard feelings. But I also told him about how grateful I was for the times I sacrificed solid things for chancier things. How even the moves that didn't pay off led to moves that did. And how grateful I was I didn't stay in my lane.

Not long after our talk, he went all in, retreating to a hunting cabin with his recording gear and musical instruments. When he emerged a long while later, he had recorded an entire album by himself.

He burned some early copies and shared them with a few trusted mentors—including me—and asked that we share our thoughts.

The music was a stark departure from his earlier work. After many listens, I told him I thought he had done the right thing. That this new sound was powerful. That his artistic instincts were leading him in a brave new direction. But then I told him there was one radical change I didn't care for. Rather than sing in his naturally rich, deep, bluesy voice, he had switched almost completely to his upper register.

"The music is great," I said. "But the falsetto? I don't think that's a great idea. I'd lose the falsetto."

He thanked me for my feedback. And then he went out and—singing in falsetto—sold millions of records and won two Grammys.

This is my favorite mentorship moment. That moment when the student overrules the teacher—not out of spite or ego, but because the teacher has helped the student come to know themself. To trust themself. This is the ultimate culmination of successful mentorship—improbable or otherwise. To break free and make your own mark, it may be necessary to reject your mentors—and put your trust in the tangents that result.

I've been there myself. I would not be typing these words if not for a man named Frank. Back in my earliest freelance days, back when I still longed to be a poet, I wrote pieces for a local magazine called *Wisconsin West*. Frank was the editor. He was also an accomplished poet and reader of poetry. He took me under his wing, recommending and sharing poetry books, spending hours helping me revise my verses, and tightening up my magazine pieces.

He taught me more about writing than any other mentor in my life.

When I signed my first book contract, the one for *Population 485*, Frank read my manuscript drafts, providing critiques and feedback. And from the first draft to the last, he was consistently bothered by my use of the word "zaftig" in the opening sentence.

Frank felt the word—derived from the Yiddish to mean "pleasantly plump"—was difficult at best, pretentious at worst. He believed readers would stumble over it—a cardinal sin impairing the flow of a smooth read.

Not only did I trust Frank's judgement, but I knew I might never have earned that book deal if not for him.

So I took "zaftig" out. Then I put it back in. Then I took it out again. And put it back in again. Draft after draft: in, out; in, out. Read the sentence to myself, read it aloud. Recited it with "zaftig" in and with "zaftig" out.

But I liked the zippy "z" sound of it. And the two-syllable rhythm of it. The *tastiness* of it. The way it so sweetly and softly fit the line. And in my earnest poet's soul, I believed it was the *right* word.

I left it in.

Two decades later, I still get notes and comments from readers reacting to "zaftig." The comments run about 90% positive, and as far as the other 10%, well, "zaftig" made a lasting impact.

All because I respected the advice of my mentor.

And then rejected it.

I hope you will do the same one day. This is not a rejection born out of petulance. It is a rejection born out of what your mentor has provided you. It is a sign that you are ready to fly solo.

To veer off the easy path and chase that tangent.

To become your own improbable mentor.

For more information, an expanded biography, or to book Mike as a speaker, please visit SneezingCow.com.

Acknowledgments

Thank you to:

First and foremost, my parents—anything decent is because of them, anything else is simply not their fault.

Andy Andrews, who discovered me in a basement, has been kind to me ever since, and planted the seed for this book while we were adrift at sea.

Thank you to Ben Shaw for his helper's heart, consultant's ear, and attorney's eye. Ben, you are uniquely suited to square up my asymmetric ways.

Joe Sanfelippo for reads and recommendations.

Tricia Duyfhuizen for lining it up and laying it out—even while laid up.

RT Vrieze for a cover that was just the ticket.

Becky and Mike for boxin'em up and shippin'em out...

And finally, to my wife and daughters, the happy tangents that keep me on course.

www.ingramcontent.com/pod-product-compliance
Lightning Source LLC
Chambersburg PA
CBHW031426120626
46545CB00006B/2287